Contents

GW00367194

SESSIONS

REFERENCE

Welcome to Growing on the Frontline

'I just wish I could be more like Jesus in everyday life.'

It's hard to argue with that. But what does it really mean? How do we become the people Jesus intends us to be, in the places we find ourselves day by day?

We want to see the fruit of the Spirit growing in us and we want to make an impact for Jesus. But reality can fall short of that, and we wonder what's getting in the way. Is God just not interested in where I spend my time – at the school gate, at work, in the queue, at the gym? Or is it me? Something about my character?

If you've engaged with LICC resources like *Fruitfulness*

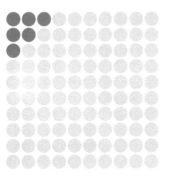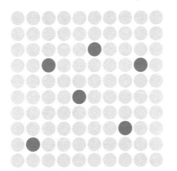

Less than 6% of people in the UK go to church monthly or more. Gathered, that feels few, but scattered in the world we can influence many people around us, as we grow more like Jesus where we are.

....

on the Frontline or *Frontline Sundays*, you'll know God is very definitely interested in the things you do every day, the places you naturally go, and the people you naturally meet. You'll know there are lots of ways to be fruitful for him. And you've probably also discovered a whole range of ways you've already been fruitful in modelling godly character, making good work, ministering grace and love... and so on.

But most of us also know there are times when we really aren't much like Jesus. When we tell the white lie, or the grey lie. When we don't do the kind thing, or the right thing. When we don't stick up for someone, or even ourselves, in the way God would want us to.

Why, we wonder, do I do things like that? What's going on inside me? And what about all the times when I don't even recognise there was a better way to respond?

Well, the good news is that our everyday contexts – our 'frontlines' – aren't just places to do things for Jesus. They're places to become more like Jesus. And *Growing on the Frontline* is designed to help you do just that – by God's grace and with his help.

It'll help you explore what's driving the choices you make when challenges and opportunities arise. And, of course, once you spot what's driving you, you can seek God's wisdom and transforming power – so that over time you'll be

more likely to respond more like Jesus, because you're becoming more like him.

In *Growing on the Frontline*, you'll engage with a combination of biblical stories and present-day examples, teaching videos, discussion questions, prayer tools, and suggestions on how to integrate what you're learning into your daily life.

As you go, you'll have the chance to be vulnerable with each other, and you might well have deeper conversations than usual. Not everyone finds this easy, but it's worth giving it a go – because when we get real with one another, it really helps the ideas we're discussing become real in our lives.

Our prayer is that you'll grow more like Jesus on your frontlines and become increasingly fruitful as you join in his kingdom work, right where you are.

Charles & Mary Hippsley
Originators of *Growing on the Frontline*

Making the most of *Growing on the Frontline*

Everything you need to get started, plus other good things to help you you use *Growing on the Frontline* in your church and keep practising what you learn.

What you'll need

1. **A copy of this guide for everyone in your group**

   Each session is built around three short videos, with discussion questions, activities, and prayer tools to help you explore that session's theme – plus ideas to try between sessions.

2. **The session videos**

   Hosted by Tim Yearsley and Ennette Lainchbury, the accompanying videos will guide you through each session, sharing biblical insight and powerful true stories.

   Available online or on DVD from **licc.org.uk/growing**.

3. **A journal**

   Get yourself a paper notebook, a suitable app, or even just a few pieces of A4! You'll be invited to use them as you go through the course.

Make a difference wherever you are

Also available

There's a whole host of great content on our website to help you get the most out of *Growing on the Frontline*.

40-day prayer journey

Perfect for after the course, get prayer prompts via email or the YouVersion app to help you embed what you've learned and keep growing.

Sermon outline

Notes and a video to help you kick off this course in a Sunday service.

Graphics pack

Graphics, slides, and posters to help you advertise *Growing on the Frontline* in your church.

Find it all at licc.org.uk/growing

SESSION 1

Growing wherever we are

Welcome to *Growing on the Frontline*! In this session, we'll explore how God can help us grow in the everyday places and situations we find ourselves, as he works through our experiences there to make us more like Jesus.

INSIGHT: FRONTLINES

Frontlines are the places and spaces we spend time, doing the things we normally do, often with people who don't know Jesus. It might be a job, a team, the local shops, your street, or your front room!

WATCH

Session 1 Part A

7 MINS

GROUP DISCUSSION   15 MINS

Discuss the following:

1. What struck you about Aisha's story?

2. Aisha found herself in a difficult situation. In what ways was it an opportunity for her to grow as a disciple? What do you think got in the way?

3. Put yourself in Aisha's shoes. What things might stop you from stepping up and having a difficult conversation in an appropriate way?

4. Where is your own frontline? Can you identify any difficult situations there that might actually be opportunities to grow and be more fruitful?

WATCH

Session 1 Part B

5 MINS

BIBLE STUDY

15 MINS

1 SAMUEL 25:14–35

Read 1 Samuel 25:14–35 together and discuss:

5. How did God present David with an opportunity to grow through this situation?

6. What do you think David learnt about himself as a result?

7. In this Bible story, David's anger could have led him astray, but Abigail's wise intervention helped him. What has helped or hindered you in growing and being fruitful on your frontline?

WATCH

Session 1
Part C

7 MINS

INSIGHT:
THE 4RS

In this resource we use a framework of four Rs to help us partner with God as we grow in maturity.

Reflecting *on our life with God and others* —

Receiving *biblical wisdom to help us develop discernment*

Reflect · Receive · Respond · Renew

Learning to **Respond** *fruitfully on our frontlines*

Being **Renewed** *so that our whole selves are more aligned with love for God and others*

PRAYER TOOL

Introducing the Examen Prayer

Examen is a silent prayer with five steps. It's about looking to the Holy Spirit, day by day, for the kind of insight Paul prays for the Philippians in Philippians 1:9–11.

Leaders: *Read out the steps below, pausing where indicated to allow one or two minutes of personal reflection.*

PREPARE
Take some slow, deep breaths and close your eyes. Begin by thanking God for everything you're grateful for today, and ask him to highlight by his Spirit what he wants you to notice as you pray and listen.

PAUSE

REVIEW
In your imagination step through your day with thankfulness, reliving any significant moments and lingering on those that seem most important.

PAUSE

CELEBRATE
Celebrate those moments when you sensed God's presence, guidance, and love. Were there times when you responded to others with love or respect, or intervened with a timely word, like Abigail in your Bible discussion?

PAUSE

REPENT
Recognise and ask God's forgiveness for any times when something got in the way of you acting fruitfully: an incident, emotion, or difficult relationship. Were there times when you let anger get the better of you, like David with Nabal?

PAUSE

LOOK AHEAD
Imagine what you'll be doing tomorrow: the tasks you have, the people you'll meet, the choices you'll make. Ask God for help with any that might be difficult or might draw you away from him.

PAUSE

Leaders: *Draw the group back together and give them an opportunity to share briefly about how they found the Examen Prayer.*

PRAY & CLOSE   5 MINS

In this session, we've explored how God can help us grow in our daily places and situations. And we've seen that it's not always enough to just know the right thing to do – we also need our hearts and will to be on board so we make good choices.

Next time we'll look more closely at the choices we make, and how they can affect our fruitfulness.

Close this session together in prayer and ask God to help you become more like Jesus in your frontline context.

BEFORE THE NEXT SESSION

Experiment with the Examen Prayer

Try using the Examen Prayer to help you notice what's going on in and around you, day by day. On page 56, you'll find suggestions for using it in different settings: in the quiet, on the move, and on your frontline.

Start a reflective journal

As you go through *Growing on the Frontline*, jot down anything you notice that feels significant. Find out more about how to journal on page 64, and use the questions below to get you started. Come ready to share your experiences when you meet next time.

- When did I give or receive love? What prompted me?

- When did I withhold love? What stopped me?

DIG DEEPER: Find helpful books, podcasts, and more on page 52

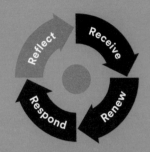

Our choices affect our fruitfulness

Last time, we explored how God can grow us to be more like Jesus in and through our daily experiences.

We also saw that just knowing the right thing to do isn't always enough on its own. In this session, we'll explore how the choices we make affect the fruit we do – or don't – bear.

OPENING QUESTIONS   5 MINS

1. Since the last session, has anyone spotted an opportunity to grow more Christlike on their frontline?

2. Has anyone had a go at using the Examen Prayer? If so, how did you get on?

WATCH

Session 2 Part A

6 MINS

GROUP DISCUSSION   10 MINS

| Discuss the following:

3. What struck you about Maria's story?

4. How did reflecting on her lack of fruitfulness make a difference to her choice?

5. Have you ever been in a similar position? What choice did you make?

ACTIVITY

Fruit and choices

Use the prompts below to reflect by yourself on the ways you're already bearing fruit, and the choices that help that fruit to grow.

Then think about where you'd like to be more fruitful, and what choices might currently be getting in the way. Refer to the 6Ms of fruitfulness to help you think about the kinds of fruit you can bear.

Fruitful areas

What are some examples of good **fruit** you're already producing on your frontline?

What **choices** help you produce that fruit?

Growth areas

What **fruit** would you like to bear but don't at the moment?

What **choices** get in the way of you bearing that fruit?

INSIGHT: THE 6MS		
	M1	Modelling godly character
	M2	Making good work
See page 17 for more detail.	**M3**	Ministering grace and love
	M4	Moulding culture
	M5	Being a Mouthpiece for truth and justice
	M6	Being a Messenger of the gospel

WATCH

**Session 2
Part B**

2 MINS

BIBLE STUDY

15 MINS

GENESIS 3:1–13

| Read Genesis 3:1–13 and discuss:

6. What struck you from the passage?

7. We know Adam and Eve made a crucial choice with disastrous consequences. But imagine you're in their place and focus on their conversation with the serpent (v1-7). What do you think might have been the thought processes behind their choice, under the surface? Why might you have done the same?

8. Now step out of character – back to being you. Pick one of the choices you identified in the 'fruit and choices' section earlier. What thought processes are you aware of that led to that choice?

INSIGHT:
CHOICES AND CONSEQUENCES

Like Adam and Eve, our choices have consequences that can go beyond what we anticipate. But we're often unaware of why we make the choices we do. Reflecting using prayer tools like Examen can help us discern what's behind our choices.

WATCH

**Session 2
Part C**

3 MINS

PRAYER TOOL

Developing the Examen Prayer

The Examen Prayer can be used in a wholly open way to review your day with God, as we did last time. And it can also be used to explore more specific aspects of your day. In this session, we'll develop our use of the Examen Prayer to reflect on the choices we've made on our frontlines.

> **Leaders:** *Read out the steps below, pausing where indicated to allow one or two minutes of personal reflection.*

PREPARE
Take a moment to make sure you are sitting comfortably. Take some slow, deep breaths and close your eyes. Begin by giving God thanks for everything that you are grateful for today and ask God by his Spirit to highlight those things that he wants you to notice as you pray and listen.

PAUSE

REVIEW
In your imagination, step through your day with thanks to God. Notice and linger over moments when you made choices on your frontline. What were you feeling as you made those decisions? Why do you think you felt that way?

PAUSE

CELEBRATE
Celebrate those moments when you sensed God's presence, guidance, and love in the choices you made.

PAUSE

REPENT
Recognise those times when something got in the way of choosing wisely, and ask for God's forgiveness.

PAUSE

LOOK AHEAD
Imagine what you might be doing tomorrow: the things you'll do, the people you'll meet, the choices you'll need to make. What might you do differently? Ask God to help you let his likeness shine through you.

PAUSE

PRAY & CLOSE

In this session, we've explored some of the ways our choices affect the fruit we bear. Next time, we'll look at what it is within us that influences those choices.

Close this session together in prayer. Pray for each other that you will make fruitful choices this week.

BEFORE THE NEXT SESSION

Keep experimenting with the Examen Prayer

Continue to use the Examen Prayer to help you reflect day by day on life on your frontline. On page 56 in this guide, you'll find suggestions for using it in different settings: in the quiet, on the move, and on your frontline itself.

Keep using your reflective journal

Make a note in your reflective journal of how you get on with the Examen Prayer and come back next time ready to share your experiences with the group. You might also find the following questions helpful as you reflect on your day or week on your frontline:

- When did I give or receive love? What choices led to fruitfulness?

- When did I withhold love? What choices prevented me from being fruitful?

DIG DEEPER: Find helpful books, podcasts, and more on page 52

THE 6MS EXPLAINED

M1 Modelling godly character

Wherever we are, we have opportunities to display the fruit of the Spirit (love, joy, peace, patience, kindness, goodness, faithfulness, gentleness, and self-control).

M2 Making good work

Whatever tasks we're doing, we seek to do them in a way that reflects our God, who creates order, generates provision, brings joy, creates beauty, and releases potential.

M3 Ministering grace and love

Just as we have received grace and love from God, we in turn show grace and love to those around us – whether we think they deserve it or not.

M4 Moulding culture

Every organisation, team, and friendship group has a 'way we do things around here'. Moulding culture is about strengthening the good and seeking kingdom ways to overcome the bad.

M5 Being a Mouthpiece for truth and justice

This could mean snuffing out gossip, making sure a colleague doesn't get wrongly blamed, changing an unfair grading system, or modifying a policy that negatively affects the vulnerable.

M6 Being a Messenger of the gospel

If we're seeking to live out the other five Ms, people are more likely to ask us questions about our faith, and the answers we give are likely to be more compelling.

See how real Christians are living out the 6Ms day by day in our '6M People' video series: **licc.org.uk/6mpeople**

SESSION 3

Our desires influence our choices

Last time we thought about the choices we make, and how those choices impact our fruitfulness.

In this session we'll explore what often lies beneath the choices we make – the desires of our hearts.

OPENING QUESTION   5 MINS

1. Has anyone been using the Examen Prayer to reflect on the choices they've been making on their frontline? If so, what have you noticed?

WATCH

**Session 3
Part A**

6 MINS

BIBLE STUDY   15 MINS

LUKE 10:25–37

| *Read Luke 10:25–37 and discuss:*

We'd probably all like to be the hero in the story, the Samaritan who shows mercy. But first, put yourself in the place of the priest or the Levite.

2. Imagine you're walking down that road, and you catch sight of that man, bloody and motionless. You slow your pace, but then look away and quicken your stride. What desires might make you want to walk past the man in need?

3. Now imagine yourself as the Good Samaritan. What convictions might motivate you to go out of your way in order to help the injured man?

Remember who Jesus was telling this story to: an expert in the Law who wanted to justify himself. Jesus told this story to prompt the expert to examine his own heart, and the desires that lay within it.

4. Think about a choice you've made recently on your frontline – it might even be one you shared last session. It could be an example of where you chose the right thing, or where you didn't. Share with the group what desire or desires you think lay beneath that choice.

WATCH

**Session 3
Part B**

5 MINS

GROUP DISCUSSION   10 MINS

5. What struck you about Anna's story?

Anna's 'unchecked desire' was to gain approval from succeeding in the work she was doing.

6. What sort of unchecked desires have you come across in yourself as you seek to serve on your frontline?

7. How might those desires hinder your ability to love and serve freely?

> **INSIGHT:
> UNCHECKED DESIRES**
>
> Desires energise us towards getting our basic needs met – like our need for approval, security, a measure of control, or a sense of purpose. If they go unchecked, self-serving desires can lead us away from God's presence and purposes.

WATCH

**Session 3
Part C**

3 MINS

PRAYER TOOL

Introducing Lectio Divina

Lectio Divina can help us engage our heart as well as our head while reading God's word. Used alongside systematic Bible study, it can help us respond prayerfully to what God might be saying to us through the text.

This prayer tool has four steps: read, listen, pray, and wait. We'll try the first three today and add the fourth step next session.

> **Leaders:** *Invite the group to quieten their thoughts and offer this time to God. Read out the steps below, pausing where indicated to allow time for personal reflection. Everyone will need to have the Bible passage in front of them.*

READ   Read through Luke 10:25–37 slowly to yourself and notice any verse or short passage that particularly stands out to you.

       PAUSE

LISTEN   Focus on that verse or passage and read it through slowly a few times, asking God to illuminate it for you. Listen for where the text connects with your life right now. What might be God's invitation to you?

       PAUSE

PRAY   Read that short verse or passage once more, continuing to listen out for how God might be speaking to you through it. Allow this Scripture to lead you into a prayerful response in your heart. As you do that, try to express your feelings honestly to God.

       PAUSE

> **Leaders:** *Encourage the group to share back what struck them as they reflected on the passage, and what difference it might make to the coming week.*

PRAY & CLOSE

5 MINS

Last time, we thought about how our choices affect our fruitfulness. In this session, we've explored how those choices are influenced by our desires. And, when they go unchecked, how that can get in the way of us loving God and others on our frontlines.

Next time, we'll be looking at how to identify some core unchecked desires, as we pay attention to what happens in everyday life using the prayer tools we've been trying together.

> **Leaders:** *close this session together with prayer, and ask God to help you notice when unchecked desires are affecting your fruitfulness.*

BEFORE THE NEXT SESSION

Try using Lectio Divina

On page 58 in this guide, you'll find suggestions for using it in different settings: in the quiet, on the move, and on your frontline itself.

Keep using your reflective journal

Make a note of the wisdom you receive from God's word that connects with your frontline context and come back next time ready to share with the group. You might also find the following questions helpful as you receive wisdom for your day or week:

- What has stood out to me as I've prayerfully read God's word?

- How has the wisdom in God's word influenced me on my frontline?

- How have my desires influenced my choices there?

> **DIG DEEPER: Find helpful books, podcasts, and more on page 52**

SESSION 4

Our emotions reveal our desires

In the last session, we saw how the choices we make in our day-to-day lives can be driven by our underlying desires. We also tried out a new prayer tool, Lectio Divina.

In this session, we'll dig deeper into the desires that influence our choices. And we'll see how we can identify some of our more powerful desires by noticing the negative emotions we feel when those unchecked desires are not being fulfilled.

OPENING QUESTION   5 MINS

1. Did anyone have a go at doing Lectio Divina by themselves? If so, how did you get on?

WATCH

Session 4 Part A

5 MINS

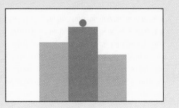

GROUP DISCUSSION   15 MINS

| Discuss the following:

2. What struck you about Chris' story?

3. How did the prayerful way Chris paid attention to his feelings help him identify his desires?

4. Think about a recent situation on your frontline that prompted a strong emotion. What did you do with that emotion? Share with the group what desire or desires you think lay beneath that choice.

5. How might you benefit from prayerfully reflecting on the emotions you feel when facing choices on your frontline?

WATCH

**Session 4
Part B**

5 MINS

BIBLE STUDY

15 MINS

MATTHEW 4:1–11

| *Read Matthew 4:1–11 and discuss:*

6. What struck you from the passage?

7. Although we're not told specifically how Jesus felt, he was clearly alert to Satan's tactics. What do you make of Jesus' response to each temptation?

8. Jesus resists the temptation to fulfil his desires for himself, but instead trusts his heavenly father. How might his approach help you in your frontline context?

WATCH

**Session 4
Part C**

7 MINS

INSIGHT: WHAT OUR EMOTIONS SAY ABOUT OUR DESIRES

We often feel negative emotions when we aren't able to fulfil our desires for ourselves. Noticing these emotions can help us discern unchecked desires.

We can feel ashamed when we don't get approval from others; we can feel afraid when our sense of security is threatened; and we can feel angry when we sense we're losing control of a situation. Anticipating any of these can also make us feel anxious.

PRAYER TOOL

Developing Lectio Divina

This time we'll use all four steps of Lectio Divina: read, listen, pray, and wait.

> **Leaders:** *Invite the group to take a moment to quieten their thoughts and offer this time to God. Read out the steps below, pausing where indicated to allow time for personal reflection. Everyone will need to have the Bible passage in front of them.*

READ Read through Matthew 4:1-11 slowly, and ask God to help you notice which of Jesus' temptations particularly speaks to you.

PAUSE

LISTEN Focus on that one short passage and read it through slowly a few times, asking God to illuminate it for you. Listen to where the text connects with your life right now. What might be God's invitation to you through what is written?

PAUSE

PRAY Read the passage once more, still listening out for how God might be speaking to you through it. Allow this Scripture to lead you into a prayerful response. As you do that identify and express your feelings honestly to God.

PAUSE

WAIT Pause and quieten your thoughts again. Silently hold what you have heard in your heart, and let the significance of God's word for you sink in.

PAUSE

> **Leaders:** *Draw the group back together and give them an opportunity to share briefly about how they found this Lectio Divina.*

PRAY & CLOSE

5 MINS

In this session, we've looked at how paying attention to our feelings can help us identify some of the unchecked desires that might be shaping our behaviour. And we've looked at three particularly powerful desires, as we thought about Chris' story, Jesus' story, and our own stories.

Next time, we'll look at the journey God takes us on as we grow in Christ – a journey through different seasons and stages, leading us into greater maturity, so we can respond to the situations we face on our frontlines more like Jesus would.

Close this session together in prayer, and ask God to help you notice your emotions and recognise the deep needs they point to – and then bring those needs to him.

BEFORE THE NEXT SESSION

Keep using Lectio Divina

Keep using Lectio Divina as part of your regular Bible reading. On page 58 in this guide, you'll find suggestions for using it in different settings: in the quiet, on the move, and on your frontline itself.

Keep using your reflective journal

Make a note in your reflective journal of anything you receive from God's word that connects with your frontline context and come back next time ready to share with the group. You might also find these questions helpful:

- What's struck me as I've prayerfully read God's word?

- How has the wisdom in God's word influenced me on my frontline?

- Have I noticed any negative emotions on my frontline? What might these indicate about my unchecked desires?

DIG DEEPER: Find helpful books, podcasts, and more on page 52

SESSION 5

Maturing in every season

In the last session, we looked at how paying attention to our emotions can help us spot the deep desires driving us.

As we start the second half of the course, we'll shift our focus from our inner life to how God helps us grow on our frontlines. In this session, we'll explore some of the different seasons of life, and how we can work with God to grow in maturity through each of these.

OPENING QUESTIONS   5 MINS

1. Has anyone been using Lectio Divina since the last session? If so, what have you received from God?

2. Have you gained any insights about your desires, and how they affect you on your frontline?

WATCH

Session 5 Part A

5 MINS

BIBLE STUDY   15 MINS

Here are some paired Bible passages with discussion questions. The first in each pair is from the early days of Peter's discipleship journey, when Jesus was physically present. The second is from months or years after Jesus had ascended.

Split into twos or threes, with each group choosing a different pair of passages to read and discuss.

Peter's growth in faith

Matthew 14:22–32: Peter tries to walk on the lake
Acts 3:1–10: Peter and John respond to a beggar

- What do you think might have changed in Peter between these two incidents?

Peter's growth in character

Mark 9:33–35: 'Who is the greatest?'
1 Peter 5:5–7: Peter's advice for relating well to others and to God

- Which unchecked desires do you recognise in these verses?

- What does Peter's advice some 30 years later suggest about how he had matured?

This conversation took place in Capernaum, where Peter's mother lived. He isn't mentioned, but it's very likely he took part.

Peter's growth in understanding of God's purposes

Matthew 16:21–23: Peter rebukes Jesus
Acts 11:1–18: God's new instructions for Peter

- In the first passage, Peter has a clear idea of what he feels God's plan for salvation should be like, but strongly disagrees with Jesus' view. In the second passage, he gradually comes to terms with the true scope of God's plans, extending to the Gentiles. What might have changed in his heart that allowed him to be more open to God's purposes?

WATCH

**Session 5
Part B**

9 MINS

GROUP DISCUSSION   10 MINS

A tree's growth is marked by rings in its trunk, produced by the passing of the seasons. Let this image and Agu's story prompt you as you discuss the following questions:

3. Which *stage* of your faith journey would you say you're in today (e.g. young sapling, established and growing, mature and fruitful tree)?

4. Which *season* do you feel you're in right now? (Use the table to help you.) How are you feeling about being in this season?

5. Have any *seasons* within your journey so far been particularly significant for your spiritual growth?

WATCH

**Session 5
Part C**

2 MINS

INSIGHT: SEASONS OF LIFE

Our walk with God is not static: it moves through a rhythm of seasons and stages as we gradually mature. Sometimes we can feel out of step when others around us are in a different season, but it's OK to be where you are right now. God works in and through each season to help us to grow.

	Signs of the season	Tasks for the season
Summer	Active in service. Exploring my call to make a difference wherever I am.	Paying attention to my thought life, dealing with unchecked desires and impulses, and beginning to develop a rhythm of prayer tools that help channel strong passions into mature patterns of growth.
Autumn	Bearing fruit, busy and productive but facing some challenges in life and perhaps starting to feel a bit tired. After a while some things may fall by the wayside.	Learning to trust when things don't go my way. Noticing how I am dealing with adversity, or too much activity. Continuing to feed on God's word and wise teaching.
Winter	Life feels less fruitful and God may seem distant. I feel stuck or frustrated; old ways are not working as well as they did, and old passions are fading.	Embracing change in my perception of God. Learning the art of waiting and trusting in the dark. Stretching out towards God even if it's hard to hear or sense him.
Spring	A deeper understanding of God and myself awakens and life seems full of potential once again.	Identifying unhelpful distractions and keeping my roots firmly planted in God – meeting my desires in him.

PRAYER TOOL

Introducing the Renewal Prayer

The Renewal Prayer is based on Paul's encouragement in Romans 12 to offer our lives as worship to him, which is only possible if our minds are renewed so we can discern God's good purposes.

It also helps us follow Paul's advice in Philippians 4:6-7 – to turn to God for our needs when we feel negative emotions and let his peace guard our hearts and minds.

Leaders: *Read out the steps below, pausing briefly where prompted to allow time for personal response.*

PREPARE **Take a few deep, slow breaths and quieten your thoughts.** Let your inward focus turn towards Jesus. You might find it helpful to speak his name quietly.

In preparation, ask the Holy Spirit to bring to mind any negative emotions you might be feeling today. Try not to analyse or reject those feelings. Simply acknowledge them.

PAUSE ▬▬▬▬▬▬▬▬▬▬▬ |

HEART Our **hearts** (like Peter's) can sometimes feel ashamed that we don't 'measure up' to others' expectations, and we can try to win their approval. Use this prayer to invite Jesus to renew your heart.

Leaders: *Invite the group to put a hand over their hearts.*

'Welcome Lord Jesus. Thank you that you love me just as I am. Please renew my heart. As I find my myself embraced by you, I entrust my need for approval to you.'

PAUSE ▬▬▬▬▬▬▬▬▬▬▬ |

MIND   When we feel threatened and afraid, our **thoughts** can be overwhelmed by disaster scenarios and by planning ways to keep ourselves safe. Use this prayer to invite Jesus to renew your mind.

> **Leaders:** *Invite the group to place a hand on the side of their heads.*

'Welcome Lord Jesus. Thank you that you are with me. Please renew my mind. As I sense your presence with me, I entrust my need for security to you.'

PAUSE

BODY   Our **bodies** often react when something threatens our ability to control what's going on around us and we get angry or frustrated: our neck or shoulders tighten, we get that 'pit of the stomach' feeling, or maybe our head starts to ache. Use this prayer to invite Jesus to renew you and bring peace to your body.

> **Leaders:** *Invite the group to place both hands on their shoulders or stomachs.*

'Welcome Lord Jesus. Thank you that you are in control. Please renew and bring peace to my body. As I sense your good purposes for me, I entrust my need for control to you.'

PAUSE

> **Leaders:** *Draw the group back together and give them an opportunity to share briefly about how they found the Renewal Prayer.*

PRAY & CLOSE

5 MINS

In this session, we've looked at the bigger picture of the journey God takes us on as we learn to grow in Christ. We've seen that we can develop greater freedom to respond to God and others in love through the stages and seasons of our faith journey.

Next time we'll focus on the winter season as a particularly challenging period but one that is really significant in our path to maturity.

Close this session together with prayer, giving thanks for the season you're in and asking God to help you to grow in it.

BEFORE THE NEXT SESSION

Try using the Renewal Prayer

Be alert to your reactions to what's happening on your frontline. Use the Renewal Prayer to ask God to help you let go of any unhelpful reactions. On page 60 in this guide, you'll find suggestions for using it in different settings: in the quiet, on the move, and on your frontline itself.

Keep using your reflective journal

Reflect on what God might be teaching you in your current season and how you are responding. Make a note in your reflective journal of anything you notice and come back next time ready to share with the group. You might also find the following questions helpful as you invite God to renew you in your day or week:

- When did I most often feel the need for security on my frontline? What did I do?

- When did I most often feel the need for approval? What did I do?

- When did I most often feel the need to control my situation? What did I do?

- What season do I sense I am in right now? How can I cooperate with God to keep growing in this season?

DIG DEEPER: Find helpful books, podcasts, and more on page 52

SESSION 6

Going deeper with God in tough times

Last time, we thought about the different stages and seasons we go through in life, and how God helps us to mature in each one. We also tried out the Renewal Prayer.

In this session, we'll dig deeper into the most challenging season, winter, and consider God's invitation to push our roots more deeply into him in this season.

OPENING QUESTIONS   5 MINS

1. Has anybody been using Renewal Prayer since the last session? Have you tried it in your frontline context?

2. Has anyone had any further thoughts on the seasons we discussed last time?

WATCH

Session 6 Part A

6 MINS

GROUP DISCUSSION   10 MINS

3. What stands out to you about the season Martin found himself in, and the way he responded to it?

4. How could things have played out if Martin had chosen to respond differently?

5. Have you ever found yourself in a winter season, when your plans didn't work out, or you lost something or someone, or you felt cut off from God or others? How did you respond? What did you learn about yourself and God?

WATCH

**Session 6
Part B**

5 MINS

BIBLE STUDY

15 MINS

HEBREWS 12:4–13

*Read Hebrews 12:4–13 together, then discuss the
following questions:*

6. What do you think is the main point, or points,
   being made in this passage?

7. In what ways could this passage help you if
   you're facing challenges on your frontline at
   the moment, or when you face them in the
   future? Consider how it could help you with:

   - Your attitude
   - The way you talk to yourself
   - The way you relate to God

WATCH

**Session 6
Part C**

5 MINS

INSIGHT: GROWTH
IN HARD TIMES

In difficult seasons of life,
there is an opportunity to
see where our spiritual
roots are truly planted. And
if we're able to recognise
God working alongside us
through the hardship and
intentionally cooperate
with him, we can grow in
maturity and capacity for
fruitfulness.

PRAYER TOOL

Applying the Renewal Prayer

Last time we used the Renewal Prayer to ask Jesus to renew us in our current season and help us to find all that we need in him. This time, we'll apply the Renewal Prayer to a particularly difficult season of life: a winter season, whether now or in the past.

Leaders: *Read out the steps below, pausing briefly in between to allow time for personal response.*

PREPARE **Take a few deep, slow breaths and quieten your thoughts.** Let your inward focus turn towards Jesus. You might find it helpful to name him to yourself.

In preparation, bring to mind a winter season of life or an event on your frontline that was particularly challenging for you. How do you remember feeling during that time? How might that emotion have been associated with, for example, your desire for approval, security, or for some measure of control?

PAUSE ⎸

We're going to hear three prayers – one about the desire for approval, one about the desire for security, and one about the desire for control. Echo one or all of them, entrusting the desire you've been thinking about to Jesus and asking him to renew you.

HEART | **Leaders:** *Invite the group to put a hand over their hearts.*

'Welcome Lord Jesus. Thank you that you love me just as I am. Please renew my heart. As I find my myself embraced by you, I entrust my need for approval to you.'

PAUSE ⎸

MIND | **Leaders:** *Invite the group to place a hand on the side of their heads.*

'Welcome Lord Jesus. Thank you that you are with me. Please renew my mind. As I sense your presence with me, I entrust my need for security to you.'

PAUSE

BODY | **Leaders:** *Invite the group to place both hands on their shoulders or stomachs.*

'Welcome Lord Jesus. Thank you that you are in control. Please renew and bring peace to my body. As I sense your good purposes for me, I entrust my need for control to you.'

PAUSE

Leaders: *Draw the group back together and give them an opportunity to share briefly about how they found the Renewal Prayer this time.*

PRAY & CLOSE

5 MINS

In this session, we've looked at some of the ways God helps us grow, particularly in the more difficult seasons or events of life.

Next time we'll be exploring how we can connect our inner growth with outward action: putting together all we've learnt so we can respond fruitfully.

Close this session together in prayer, taking the opportunity to pray for anyone currently experiencing a difficult season.

BEFORE THE NEXT SESSION

Continue using the Renewal Prayer

Use the Renewal Prayer to keep inviting God to help you grow in freedom from unchecked desires. On page 60 in this guide, you'll find suggestions for using it in different settings: in the quiet, on the move, and on your frontline itself.

Keep using your reflective journal

Continue reflecting on hard seasons you've experienced. What do you notice about your response in those times? How have you grown through them? Make a note in your reflective journal. You might also find the following questions helpful:

- When did I face a challenge on my frontline this week?

- Where did I go for the inner resources to respond?

- What might that tell me about where my spiritual roots are planted?

DIG DEEPER: Find helpful books, podcasts, and more on page 52

SESSION 7

Turning inner growth into fruitful action

Last time, we thought about winter seasons. We observed that though they aren't always easy, God's invitation is to push deeper into him and mature through them.

This session is about putting together all we've learnt so we can grow in freedom from unchecked desires and respond fruitfully.

OPENING QUESTIONS   5 MINS

1. Has anyone had any further thoughts on the things we discussed last time about winter seasons?

2. Has anybody been using the Renewal Prayer on your frontline? If so, what difference has it made?

WATCH

Session 7 Part A

5 MINS

GROUP DISCUSSION   10 MINS

3. What's struck you about Priya's story so far?

4. How might *you* have been tempted to respond to that angry parent if you were in her situation?

5. What kind of response would most likely have led to a fruitful outcome?

WATCH

**Session 7
Part B**

6 MINS

BIBLE STUDY

15 MINS

JAMES 3:13–18

Read James 3:13–18 together, then discuss:

6. What stood out to you from this passage?

7. James mentions envy and selfish ambition:
   two of the negative results of trying to fulfil
   our desires for security, approval, or control
   by ourselves. Which unchecked desire do you
   notice most often when you 'look in the mirror'?

8. What might help you to be mindful of this
   on your frontline, and enable you to 'sow in
   peace' (v18)?

WATCH

**Session 7
Part C**

5 MINS

PRAYER TOOL

Introducing the PAUSE Prayer

Our unchecked desires can often influence our actions without us noticing. But if we stay alert to our reactions on our frontlines, there's an opportunity to respond more fruitfully. The PAUSE Prayer can help us interrupt the momentum of our unchecked desires and turn to God

> **Leaders:** *Read out the following introduction and the steps of the PAUSE Prayer, allowing time in between each for personal response.*

Think of a recent situation when you were anxious about what to do, or reacting strongly in an unhelpful way. Keep that situation in mind as we step through the PAUSE Prayer.

PAUSE	You're already pausing by engaging in this exercise! So just pay attention to what actually happened, without placing blame, and ask God to give you insight as you go through this prayer.
ACKNOWLEDGE	Run through what happened in your mind. How did you feel at the time? Name that feeling honestly before God, without judging or justifying it.
UNDERSTAND	What do the facts of the situation and your feelings at the time tell you about your underlying desires? Remember fear often links to a desire for safety or security; shame links to a desire for approval; and anger links to a desire for some measure of control.
SURRENDER	If you recognise an unchecked desire that was driving you in that situation, invite Jesus to renew you and help you find what you need in him.
ENGAGE	Prayerfully place the outcome and yourself in God's hands. Ask for godly wisdom to be able to respond well the next time you face a situation like that on your frontline.

> **Leaders:** *Draw the group back together and give them an opportunity to share briefly about how they found the PAUSE Prayer.*

PRAY & CLOSE

In this session, we've looked at how we can grow in the freedom to respond well to people and situations by dealing with our unchecked desires and responding with godly wisdom.

Next time we'll be exploring some ways in which we can embed what we've been learning, to sustain our growth and fruitfulness.

Close this session together in prayer, taking a moment to name your frontlines and ask God to help you be attentive to him and respond well to others there.

BEFORE THE NEXT SESSION

Practise the PAUSE Prayer

Practise the PAUSE Prayer by yourself and try putting it into action on your frontline. The more you use it, the more natural you'll find it when the moment comes in a busy day. You can find tips on using it on your frontline on page 62 in this guide. Next time, come ready to share how you got on.

Keep using your reflective journal

You might find the following questions helpful as you respond to God and others in your day or week:

- When did I react strongly to a person or situation on my frontline?

- What happened? Did I find myself carried along by my reaction? Was I able to PAUSE and respond in love?

- What did I learn?

DIG DEEPER: Find helpful books, podcasts, and more on page 52

SESSION 8

Sustaining growth on the frontline

Last time we thought about how we can respond well to situations on our frontlines. We saw how the PAUSE Prayer can help us grow in this area.

In this final session we'll explore how we can embed what we've been learning throughout this course, looking at three ways we can grow and be fruitful over the long haul.

OPENING QUESTIONS   5 MINS

1. How have you noticed yourself responding differently this week to opportunities on your frontline as a result of the things we've learned?

2. Has anyone had a go at using the PAUSE Prayer? If so, can you share your story of what happened?

WATCH

Session 8 Part A

5 MINS

GROUP DISCUSSION   10 MINS

3. Can you think of a time when you responded well to an opportunity to be fruitful on your frontline (perhaps living out one or more of the 6Ms)? Share your stories with each other.

4. What effect has that positive experience of being fruitful had on how you've faced similar opportunities since then?

WATCH

**Session 8
Part B**

5 MINS

BIBLE STUDY

15 MINS

ROMANS 12:1–21

Read Romans 12:1–21 together, paying particular attention to the situations described in verses 9–21. Then discuss the following questions:

6. What strikes you about the responses Paul encourages the Roman Christians to make?

7. Have you faced any similar situations in your frontline context?

8. Bearing in mind what we've covered in this course, how might the renewing of your mind, discernment of God's purposes, and a clear assessment of yourself (v1–3) make it easier for you to respond fruitfully there?

WATCH

**Session 8
Part C**

6 MINS

INSIGHT: KEYS TO SUSTAINING FRUITFULNESS

To help you keep growing on your frontline, remember:

1. When you act fruitfully on your frontline, it reinforces your internal growth

2. You can practise acting fruitfully in your Christian community and then take it into the community on your frontline

3. Using prayer tools that you find helpful regularly can help create a healthy rhythm of engagement with God as you choose how to act

ACTIVITY

Fruit and roots

This final reflection is an opportunity for you to look at your own frontline story and draw together the ideas we've explored in *Growing on the Frontline*.

> **Leaders:** *Take the group through this reflection step by step, allowing time in between for people to write down what they discover.*

- Looking at the tree on page 47, remind yourself of the sort of fruit you'd like to bear on your frontline (you might like to look back at your notes from session 2 and the 6Ms on page 17). Write these next to the apples.

- Which core needs (for example, for security, approval, or a measure of control) have you identified as particularly significant for you? Write these next to the roots.

When these needs ignite strong desires and we seek to satisfy them for ourselves rather than in God, they can grow unchecked and interfere with our capacity to love God and others.

- What prayer tools help you keep your roots firmly planted in God and to trust him for your legitimate needs? They could be ones we've tried during this course, or others you find life-giving. Write these next to the soil beneath the tree.

> **Leaders:** *Draw the group back to discuss:*

- Which prayer tools have you found the most helpful with the process of **reflecting, receiving, renewing and responding**?

- How could you use them in a sustainable daily or weekly rhythm, to help you keep growing on your frontline?

How I want to be fruitful:

-
-
-

Core needs:

-
-
-

Prayer practices:

-
-
-

PRAY & CLOSE

As you finish this course, offer yourselves in service to God on your frontlines and ask him to help you grow in wisdom, discernment, and greater fruitfulness there.

You could pray for each other as a sign of your commitment to pursuing growth, maturity, and fruitfulness, using this adaptation of Paul's prayer for the Philippian church.

'May your love abound more and more in knowledge and depth of insight, so that you may be able to discern what is best and may be pure and blameless for the day of Christ, filled with the fruit of righteousness that comes through Jesus Christ – to the glory and praise of God.'

Philippians 1:9–11

AFTER THE COURSE

The growing doesn't stop here! As you go about your daily life:

Establish a rhythm of prayer

Establish a rhythm using prayer tools that helps you reflect, receive God's wisdom, be renewed, and respond well.

Check in from time to time

Remember to check in from time to time, encourage each other, and share what you see God doing in and through you on your frontlines (turn over the page for ideas on how to do this!).

Continue to keep a reflective journal

You might find the following questions helpful as you continue to grow on your frontline going on from here:

- What did I learn about myself and God today?

- What difference did God's wisdom make to what I said or did?

- What did I do with any unchecked desires that I recognised?

- How did I respond to the situations and people on my frontline?

Find a mentor

Some people find it helpful to seek the wisdom of a more mature Christian to accompany them on their walk with God – encouraging them to keep growing.

One option is to find a Spiritual Director: someone who listens deeply to what you share about your walk with God, and helps you discern his invitation to grow. Many Anglican dioceses offer this service, or you can find a list of trained directors at **lcsd.org.uk**

DIG DEEPER: Find helpful books, podcasts, and more on page 52

Helping each other keep growing

Growing on the Frontline might be an eight-session course, but reaching maturity in Christ takes a lifetime!

We recommend you plan in some regular times to help each other keep growing. Think of them as routine check-ups: moments to see how far you've come and think about what needs some work.

Here's a suggested plan for the year after *Growing on the Frontline* – feel free to adapt it or come up with your own.

Three months on:

Reflect

- Revisit the Examen Prayer together as a group and spend some time talking through what you have been noticing about yourself, God, and others on your frontlines

- Put together a framework to help you organise your life around a healthy set of practices. You can find tips at **practicingtheway.org/ unhurry**

- To go deeper, read *Reimagining the Ignatian Examen* by Mark E. Thibodeaux and discuss what struck you

Six months on:
Receive

- Pick a passage to study together as a group, using Lectio Divina to reflect on it deeply and asking God to speak to you about your daily context through it

- Make sure that you connect your regular Bible readings with life on your frontline and seek God's wisdom for that context

- To go deeper, work through one (or several!) of LICC's *Gateway Seven Series* of Bible studies as a group to explore Scripture's relevance for daily life. Find them at **licc.org.uk/ gatewayseven**

Nine months on:
Renew

- Take some time to review together how your awareness of God, yourself and others has changed over the last few months:

  - How do you see this in your small group?
  - How do you see this on your frontlines?

- Share any breath prayers you've found helpful with each other

- To go deeper, read *The Gift of Being Yourself* by David G. Benner, and discuss what was most meaningful to you together as a group

One year on:
Respond

- Talk together about how you have found 'PAUSE-ing' on your frontline

- Choose two of LICC's 6M People video series to watch. Find them at **licc.org.uk/6mpeople.**

  Talk them over together:

  - What fruitful choices and behaviours most stood out to you in the videos you watched?
  - Thinking about your own frontlines, where can you see yourselves being fruitful?
  - Is anything getting in the way?
  - What's that telling you about yourself and how might you respond differently?

RESOURCES

Dig Deeper

If you'd like to go deeper, these great books, podcasts, apps, and blogs will help you explore the themes covered in each session of *Growing on the Frontline* in more detail. Some particularly helpful books appear more than once. For those, we've indicated which chapters are most relevant to which sessions.

SESSION 1

6M People video series
LICC, 2021
licc.org.uk/6mpeople

Fruitfulness on the Frontline
by Mark Greene
IVP, 2014
licc.org.uk/fruitfulness

Becoming More Like Christ
by Peter R Holmes and Susan B Williams
Authentic Media, 2007

Spirituality Workbook
David Runcorn
SPCK, 2006

SESSION 2

Emotionally Healthy Spirituality
(Updated Version)
by Peter Scazzero
Zondervan, 2014
Chapter 2

Emotionally Healthy Leader Podcast
'Part 1 | The Problem of Emotionally Unhealthy Spirituality'
with Pete Scazzero
2015–2022

Atlas of the Heart
by Brené Brown
Vermilion, 2021

Unlocking Us Podcast
'Atlas of the Heart, Audience Q&A, Part 1 of 2'
with Brené Brown, Ashley Brown Ruiz, & Barrett Guillen
May 18, 2022

Anatomy of the Soul
by Curt Thompson
Tyndale House, 2010
Chapter 11

Being Known Podcast
with Curt Thompson, MD and Pepper Sweeney
2021–2022

Reimagining the Examen App
Loyola Press, 2018

SESSION 3

Befriending our Desires
(Third Edition)
by Philip Sheldrake
Liturgical Press, 2016
Chapters 1, 5

The Psychology of Christian Character Formation
by Joanna Collicutt
SCM Press, 2015
Chapters 1–3

Emotionally Healthy Spirituality
(Updated Version)
by Peter Scazzero
Zondervan, 2014
Chapter 1

**Emotionally Healthy
Leader Podcast**
'Part 8 | Grow Into
Emotionally Mature Adult'
with Pete Scazzero
2015–2022

SESSION 4

Earthed in God
Christopher Chapman
Canterbury Press, 2018
Chapters 8–9

Resilience in Life and Faith
Tony Horsfall and
Debbie Hawker
BRF, 2019
Chapters 7–8

Atlas of the Heart
Brené Brown
Vermilion, 2021

SESSION 5

Spiritual Rhythm
Mark Buchanan
Zondervan, 2010
Chapters 1–9

The Critical Journey
Janet O Hagberg and
Robert A Guelich
Sheffield Publishing, 2005

Earthed in God
Christopher Chapman
Canterbury Press, 2018

SESSION 6

Resilience in Life and Faith
Tony Horsfall and
Debbie Hawker
BRF, 2019
Chapters 6, 14

**Emotionally Healthy
Spirituality**
(Updated Version)
by Peter Scazzero
Zondervan, 2014
Chapters 4–5

**Emotionally Healthy
Leader Podcast**
'Part 5 | Enlarge Your Soul
Through Grief and Loss'
with Pete Scazzero
2015–2022

Spiritual Rhythm
Mark Buchanan
Zondervan, 2010
Chapters 1–2

SESSION 7

Anatomy of the Soul
by Curt Thompson
Tyndale House, 2010
Chapters 4–6

Renovation of the Heart
(20th Anniversary Edition)
Dallas Willard
Form, 2021
Chapters 6–8

**The Psychology of
Christian Character
Formation**
by Joanna Collicutt
SCM Press, 2015
Chapters 4–6

SESSION 8

**Emotionally Healthy
Spirituality**
(Updated Version)
by Peter Scazzero
Zondervan, 2014
Chapters 7–8

**Emotionally Healthy
Leader Podcast**
'Part 9 | Develop a
"Rule Of Life"'
with Pete Scazzero
2015–2022

Renovation of the Heart
(20th Anniversary Edition)
Dallas Willard
Form, 2021
Chapters 10–12

Earthed in God
by Christopher Chapman
Canterbury Press, 2018
Chapters 10–12

Using prayer tools to help you grow

Prayer tools are simple ways you can connect with God regularly throughout your day or your week.

Christians have been using a whole range of prayer tools like these since the days of the early church. Think of them as ideas to try: helpful pointers for how you might bring your daily ups and downs to God, and invite him to help you respond like Christ.

How do they help?

Prayer tools can help us grow more sensitive to God, give us regular moments to respond to his word, and help us cooperate with the Holy Spirit as he transforms us to be more like Christ.

That transformation doesn't happen overnight, and prayer tools won't make us more Christlike all by themselves! But they can provide moments to be inwardly shaped by God – so we can look outwards and see the needs of others with fresh eyes and a new freedom to act.

Think of it like looking after house plants. You're not the one who makes an aloe vera grow, but you do give it good soil, light, and water so it has the best chance of maturing. Prayer tools do the same thing for us – giving us what we need to grow through intentional interaction with God.

How do I use them?

In *Growing on the Frontline*, you've tried out four different prayer tools:

- **EXAMEN PRAYER**
  A much-loved tool used by Christians for centuries to help them reflect on everyday life with God

- **LECTIO DIVINA**
  An approach to reading Scripture passed down from the early church, that helps you engage your heart and your head in listening to God's word

- **RENEWAL PRAYER**
  A simple way to handle our emotions prayerfully, inviting God to renew our hearts, bodies, and minds

- **PAUSE PRAYER**
  A practical tool to help you pause in the moment, acknowledge, understand, and surrender your reactions to God, and then engage those around you with love

In between sessions, you'll have the chance to try each one on your own. Not just when you can be quiet and focused, but also in your daily life: on the go and on your frontline.

The next few pages are full of ideas to help you do that. Give them a go and see what works for you! You don't have to suddenly fill your diary with prayer time – the goal is just to build a habit or two that help realign your perspective with God's, day to day.

After a few days using each prayer tool, use these questions to reflect on how you've got on:

- How helpful did I find this prayer tool?

- How likely am I to use it in future?

- What did I notice about myself as I did it?

- Did I see any differences on my frontline as a result?

EXAMEN PRAYER

In the quiet

| *Find a comfortable spot where you won't be disturbed for 10 minutes or so.*

PREPARE
Take some slow, deep breaths to become 'present' in the moment. Begin by giving God thanks and ask him to highlight the things he wants you to notice as you pray and listen.

REVIEW
Step through your day, reliving any significant moments and focusing on any that seem most important. Notice how you felt: were you drawn towards or away from God? Why?

CELEBRATE
Celebrate when you sensed God's presence, guidance, and love. Were there times when you responded to others with love? Lift your hands in celebration and thanksgiving.

REPENT
Recognise when something got in the way of fruitfulness, and ask God's forgiveness for how you acted in that moment. Bow your head in acknowledgement and to receive God's mercy.

LOOK AHEAD
Imagine what you'll be doing tomorrow. Ask God for help with any tasks, people, or choices that might be difficult or might draw you away from him.

On the move

This QR code and link go to an audio guide to lead you through the Examen on the move.

Audio guide: licc.org.uk/growing-audio

As well as praying through the steps, try engaging your senses:

- Take some deep breaths in through your nose at the start. What do you smell? How does that help locate you in the present moment?

- If you're walking, imagine yourself going through your day: getting to your frontline, walking through your time there, and leaving. Pray as you walk through those moments.

On your frontline

You may not have time for a lengthy reflection on your frontline, but it can still be really helpful to have a short reminder to help you reflect 'live' on the things happening around you.

Spread your Examen Prayer over the time you're on your frontline using these three short questions:

Arriving
Where are the opportunities to bless others today?

Mid-way
When have I given love? When have I withheld love?

Leaving
What did I learn about myself and God today?

AUDIO GUIDE

LECTIO DIVINA

In the quiet

Find a comfortable spot where you won't be disturbed for 10 minutes or so. Choose a Bible passage to focus on – maybe one that's struck you recently, or just one that jumps off the page.

PREPARE — Take some slow, deep breaths to become 'present' in the moment. Sit quietly in God's presence and let your focus rest on him. Then ask God to speak to you through the passage you have chosen.

READ — **Read the passage slowly** – out loud if you can. Let the words resonate in your heart, and hold a hand over your heart. If a phrase or word stands out to you, stop and reflect on it before moving on.

LISTEN — **Read the passage again**, focusing on the part that struck you. Ask God to show you its significance for you. Notice what feelings, images, or memories might also stir in you. What is God's invitation to you in those words? As you listen, hold your hands out in an attitude of receiving.

PRAY — **Read the passage a third time** and talk with God about what you've noticed. Share your honest response with God. How do you feel about the text? What has brought life to you? Do you sense any resistance or push-back in yourself?

WAIT — Close by sitting in silence in God's presence for a few minutes, with hands folded in your lap. Hold what you have heard in your heart, and let the significance of God's word for you sink in. There's no need to say anything.

You might want to jot something down as a reminder of what you've received and take it with you into the coming day.

On the move

This QR code and link go to an audio guide to lead you through the Lectio Divina on the move.

Audio guide: licc.org.uk/growing-audio

If it's hard to read your chosen Bible passage on the go, try listening instead using an app like YouVersion. Audio is available for many of the more popular Bible versions on this app.

AUDIO GUIDE

On your frontline

If you did Lectio Divina in the quiet this morning or last night, you can keep engaging with the passage on your frontline.

Arriving

Jot down the significant words you noticed on a post-it note or a phone reminder.

Mid-way

Ask yourself 'How is God's wisdom in those words connecting with my life today?'

Leaving

Consider what difference this godly wisdom made to you – or through you to others on your frontline.

RENEWAL PRAYER

In the quiet

Find a comfortable spot where you won't be disturbed for 10 minutes or so.

PREPARE
Take a few deep, slow breaths and quieten your thoughts. Let your inward focus turn towards Jesus. You might find naming him helpful.

REMEMBER
You might already be carrying a negative emotion. If not, ask the Holy Spirit to help you remember a recent time when you reacted negatively to someone or something. Try to simply recognise that emotion rather than judging or justifying it. Use the prayer(s) below that are most appropriate to that emotion.

HEART
Our hearts can sometimes feel ashamed that we don't 'measure up' to others' expectations.

Welcome Lord Jesus. Thank you that you love me just as I am. Please renew my heart. [Place a hand over your heart.] As I find my myself embraced by you, I entrust my need for approval to you.

HEAD
When we feel threatened and afraid, our thoughts can be overwhelmed by disaster scenarios.

Welcome Lord Jesus. Thank you that you are with me. Please renew my mind. [Place a hand on the side of your head.] As I sense your presence with me, I entrust my need for security to you.

BODY
Our bodies often react when something threatens our ability to control what's going on around us and we get angry or frustrated.

Welcome Lord Jesus. Thank you that you are in control. Please renew and bring peace to my body. [Place both hands on your shoulders or over your stomach.] As I sense your good purposes for me, I entrust my need for control to you.

On the move

This QR code and link go to an audio guide to lead you through the Renewal Prayer on the move.

Audio guide: **licc.org.uk/growing-audio**

AUDIO GUIDE

On your frontline

'Breath prayers' are a quick way to use this approach on your frontline, helping you reconnect to God and his provision whenever you become aware of a negative emotion.

Simply pray one short phrase of Scripture on the in-breath and one on the out-breath, repeating as often as you want.

Choose breath prayer phrases that are meaningful to you personally. You could try using some of the Scripture that's struck you from Lectio Divina – or to get you started, here are examples that relate to some of the core emotions and desires:

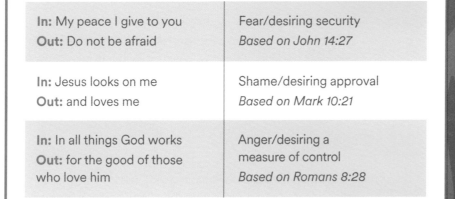

In: My peace I give to you **Out:** Do not be afraid	Fear/desiring security *Based on John 14:27*
In: Jesus looks on me **Out:** and loves me	Shame/desiring approval *Based on Mark 10:21*
In: In all things God works **Out:** for the good of those who love him	Anger/desiring a measure of control *Based on Romans 8:28*

PAUSE PRAYER

In the quiet

The PAUSE Prayer is designed to be used on your frontline, but it's helpful to practise in the quiet.

Recall a recent incident that created a strong reaction in you, perhaps one in which you felt you could have responded better.

PAUSE — Imagine the incident you have in mind has just happened. What might help you to press the hold button? Think about what happened, without apportioning blame, and ask God to give you insight as you step through the prayer

ACKNOWLEDGE — Run through the incident in your mind. How do you feel about it? Name that feeling honestly before God without judging or justifying it.

UNDERSTAND — What do the facts of the situation and what you felt about them tell you about your unchecked desires? Fear often links to a desire for safety or security; shame links to a desire for approval; and anger links to a desire for some measure of control.

SURRENDER — If you recognise an unchecked desire driving you in that situation, invite Jesus to renew you and help you find what you need in him.

ENGAGE — Is there anything you need to do about the incident you've been thinking about? Prayerfully place the outcome and yourself in God's hands. Ask for wisdom to know how to respond well the next time you face something similar on your frontline.

On the move

This QR code and link go to an audio guide to lead you through the PAUSE Prayer on the go.

If you're on your commute to your frontline, this can be a good time to rehearse the PAUSE Prayer in anticipation of any opportunities or difficult situations you know you might find when you get there.

Audio guide: **licc.org.uk/growing-audio**

AUDIO GUIDE

On your frontline

Once you've developed 'muscle memory' by practising on your own, the PAUSE Prayer is perfect for use in the moment on your frontline, as you encounter challenges and opportunities for fruitfulness.

PAUSE	*How are you reacting?*
ACKNOWLEDGE	*How are you feeling about what's happening?*
UNDERSTAND	*What desire is stopping you from being fruitful?*
SURRENDER	*Entrust it to Jesus and ask him to renew you.*
ENGAGE	*Act out of love for the people concerned.*

KEEPING A REFLECTIVE JOURNAL

Our day-to-day lives provide lots of opportunities to grow as disciples. But they're easy to miss if we don't take time to reflect with God!

That's where journaling comes in. Essentially, it's a good way of paying attention and noticing what God wants us to notice on our frontlines.

Over time, it can help you see what he's been teaching you in and through your daily experiences – perhaps a knee-jerk response he's challenging you to surrender, or a gift he's encouraging you to use more.

You don't have to just write! You could also draw pictures to articulate how you feel, or include photos, videos, or audio if you're journaling on your phone. However you express yourself, do it prayerfully in the presence of God, and be open to his inspiration and wisdom.

As you go through the course, try journaling at least once a week, particularly when something significant has happened. You can use the space however you want.

Journaling questions

If you'd appreciate something to get you started, here are a few questions to kick off with.

- What conversations have I had on my frontline today?

- Does anything that's happened today stand out as particularly significant?

- What have I noticed about myself?

- What have I noticed about God?

- Are there Christlike habits or behaviour I'd like to strengthen?

- Are there unhelpful habits or behaviour I'd like to stop?

MORE RESOURCES FOR YOUR CHURCH

Energise your whole church with *Frontline Sundays*

Imagine if every Christian in your church asked God, 'How do you want me to be good news to the people around me every day?' And imagine if every Sunday equipped them for that mission out in his world. *Frontline Sundays* provides everything you need to run five services that will affirm and inspire your congregation for everyday mission.

licc.org.uk/frontlinesundays

Do *Fruitfulness on the Frontline* with your small group

The previous resource in this series will help you explore in depth what fruitfulness looks like for you on your frontline, and encourage one another as you seek to live with and for Christ right where you are. This eight-session study is brimming with real-life stories, biblical insight, and practical tips.

licc.org.uk/fruitfulness

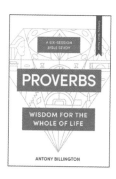

Explore the Bible with *The Gateway Seven Series*

Grow your confidence in the Bible's relevance to your daily life with these beautiful studies. Covering seven Bible books, each from a different genre, they'll deepen your reading of Scripture and open up new applications for your whole life.

licc.org.uk/gatewayseven

licc.

The London Institute for Contemporary Christianity

Imagine if every Christian lived their life as Jesus would.

It would transform the people and places around them. It would change their organisations, communities, and societies. And it would change the world – as God works in and through his people, right where they are.

But most Christians tell us they have neither the vision nor the tools for the task. That's where LICC comes in. We're working to catalyse a movement that empowers Christians to live as disciples of Jesus in daily life.

We're here to help people know God more deeply, and bring his wisdom, grace, and truth to the things they do – at work, at college, and at home; in the pub, the shops, and the gym; on social media, in the office, and out with friends.

We work with individuals, church leaders, and those who train them, partnering with organisations and networks across the denominations. We delve into the Bible, think hard about contemporary culture, and listen carefully to God's people, exploring the challenges and opportunities they face.

What we do comes out of what we learn. Resources, events, training, articles, books, films, stories, and more – all designed to encourage whole-life discipleship.

Jesus calls people into a movement of hope that will bring life to every human being and the entire planet. Today, the need for disciples living out that hope day by day is as great as ever.

We're working to engage over a million Christians with this whole-life vision.

Discover how you can get involved at **licc.org.uk**